Living in Style
New York

Photographs by Reto Guntli

teNeues

© 2010 teNeues Verlag GmbH & Co. KG, Kempen
Photographs © 2010 Reto Guntli
All photographs courtesy of zapaimages (www.zapaimages.com)
All rights reserved.

Text written by Joshua M. Bernstein
Editorial Coordination by Maria Regina Madarang
Design by Robb Ogle
French Translation and Proofreading by Helena Solodky-Wang
German Translation by Carmen E. Berelson
Italian Translation by Elisabetta Mazzantini-Clark, Italian Proofreading by Don Clark except where noted
Italian Translation and Proofreading for "Skyline Views," "Pop Modernist Style," "Upper East Side
    Luxury," and "Bohemian Treasure" by Gloria Bianchi
Spanish Translation and Proofreading by Diego Mansilla except where noted
Spanish Translation and Proofreading for "Skyline Views," "Pop Modernist Style," "Upper East Side
    Luxury," and "Bohemian Treasure" by Beatriz Álvarez
Production by Nele Jansen
Color Separations by Fischer Graphische Produktionen GmbH

Published by teNeues Publishing Group

teNeues Verlag Gmbh + Co. KG
Am Selder 37
47906 Kempen
Germany
Tel.: 0049-(0)2152-916-0
Fax: 0049-(0)2152-916-111
E-mail: books@teneues.de

teNeues Publishing Company
16 West 22nd Street
New York, NY 10010
USA
Tel.: 001-212-627-9090
Fax: 001-212-627-9511

teNeues Publishing UK Ltd.
21 Marlowe Court, Lymer Avenue
London, SE19 1LP
Great Britain
Tel.: 0044-208-670-7522
Fax: 0044-208-670-7523

teNeues France S.A.R.L.
39, rue de Billets
18250 Henrichemont
France
Tel.: 0033-2-48269348
Fax: 0033-1-70723482

Press department: arehn@teneues.de
Tel.: 0049-(0)2152-916-202

www.teneues.com
ISBN: 978-3-8327-9380-7
Printed in China

MANHATTAN

THE HAMPTONS

UPSTATE NEW YORK

BIOGRAPHIES & CREDITS

Introduction

In the hustling, bustling, multicultural city of 8,274,527 (give or take a couple) highly opinionated souls, few topics dominate New Yorkers' daily conversations quite like the subject of home.

Like anything else in this metropolis, creating a great home doesn't come easy. The city's apartments are legendarily miniscule, or they're so ancient that they require a floor-to-rafters restoration. Instead of being deterred by these roadblocks, endless waves of intrepid homeowners, architects and designers have taken up the challenge. But in a sky-scraping metropolis as grand as New York, hastily hammered renovations and Ikea-quality interiors will simply not pass muster. No, this town demands habitats as stunning, luxurious and awe-inspiring as the glittering city itself. The homes need not cost tens of millions of dollars, but they should definitely look like they do.

From the towering, tasteful townhouses of Harlem to the sun-soaked lofts of arty Soho, these lavish homes are effortlessly bold, chic and unique, doubling as museum-worthy works of art. And though these extravagant New York dwellings are as idiosyncratic as fingerprints, they share one common, defining trait: they're a home.

Einleitung

In der geschäftigen, brodelnden, multikulturellen Stadt mit ziemlich genau 8.274.527 Einwohnern, die von ihrer Meinung überzeugt sind, gehört das Thema Wohnen bei New Yorkern zu den wichtigsten Gesprächsthemen.

Genauso wie alles andere in dieser Metropole, ist es nicht einfach, ein wirklich überwältigendes Zuhause zu schaffen. Die Apartments der Stadt sind bekanntlich winzig oder sie sind so alt, dass sie einer Totalüberholung bedürfen. Ganze Armeen von Eigenheimbesitzern, Architekten und Designern lassen sich dadurch nicht abschrecken, sondern stellen sich der Problematik. In einer in den Himmel reichenden Weltstadt mit der Grandesse von New York sind eilig durchgeführte Renovierungen und Innenausstattungen im Stil von Ikea einfach nicht akzeptabel. Nein, diese Stadt verlangt Lebensräume, die ebenso atemberaubend, luxuriös und überwältigend sind wie die glitzernde Stadt selbst. Die Eigenheime müssen nicht viele Millionen Dollar kosten, aber sie müssen ganz sicher so aussehen.

Von den imposanten, geschmackvollen Reihenhäusern von Harlem bis zu den lichtdurchfluteten Lofts des Künstlerviertels Soho – diese großartigen Behausungen vermitteln den Eindruck eines mühelosen Schicks und einer beiläufigen Individualität und sind gleichzeitig Kunstwerke von Museumsqualität. Diese extravaganten New Yorker Apartments sind so individuell wie Fingerabdrücke. Allerdings haben sie ein Charakteristikum, das ihnen gemein ist: Sie sind ein Zuhause.

Introduction

Dans cette ville multiculturelle, animée et tourbillonnant d'activités, où 8 274 527 (à quelque chose près) d'esprits sont prêts à avoir des opinions passionnés sur tout, peu de sujets domine les conversations quotidiennes des New Yorkais comme le thème de la maison.

Comme tout ce qui existe dans cette mégalopole, ce n'est pas facile de créer un chez soi qui en vaille la peine. Les appartements de la ville ont à juste titre la réputation d'être minuscules ou ils sont tellement vieux qu'il faut les restaurer du sol au plafond. Au lieu d'être découragées par ces barrages, des vagues incessantes de propriétaires, architectes et décorateurs intrépides sont venues relever le défi. Mais dans une mégalopole de gratte-ciels de la taille de New York, des rénovations ficelées à la hâte ou des intérieurs style Ikea ne tiennent pas la route. Non, la ville demande des intérieurs aussi époustouflants, luxueux à vous couper le souffle comme la cité qui resplendit de mille feux. Les demeures n'ont pas besoin de couter des dizaines de millions de dollars mais elles doivent définitivement en donner l'apparence.

Des maisons mitoyennes de bon gout, toute en hauteur de Harlem aux lofts inondés de soleil du quartier des arts de Soho, ces résidences somptueuses sont au premier coup d'œil audacieuses, chics et uniques, des véritables œuvres d'art dignes d'un musée. Et bien que ces intérieurs extravagants de New York soient aussi uniques que des empreintes digitales, ils ont un trait commun bien défini : on est chez soi.

Introducción

En la dinámica, bulliciosa y multicultural ciudad donde viven 8.274.527 (más o menos una o dos) muy dogmáticas almas, pocos asuntos dominan las conversaciones diarias de los neoyorquinos tanto como el tema de la vivienda.

Nada es fácil en esta metrópolis, y crear un hogar de categoría no es una excepción. Los apartamentos de la ciudad son legendariamente minúsculos, o son tan antiguos que necesitan una restauración de piso a techo. Lejos de ser disuadidos por estos obstáculos, incesantes olas de intrépidos propietarios, arquitectos y diseñadores han aceptado el desafío. Pero en una metrópolis tan grande como Nueva York, con inmensos rascacielos, las renovaciones precipitadas y los interiores de calidad Ikea sencillamente no son aceptables. No, esta ciudad exige hábitats tan deslumbrantes, lujosos y formidables como la misma rutilante ciudad. Las viviendas no necesitan costar decenas de millones de dólares, pero definitivamente deben aparentar que lo valen.

Desde las casas adosadas (townhouses) de Harlem, imponentes y de gusto exquisito, hasta los luminosos lofts del artístico Soho, todas estas espléndidas viviendas son llamativas, elegantes y a la vez piezas de arte dignas de un museo. Y aunque estas extravagantes viviendas de Nueva York son tan personales como una huella digital, todas comparten un rasgo que las define: constituyen un hogar.

Introduction

Nel trambusto di una città indaffarata e multiculturale di 8.274.527 anime (una più, una meno), ognuna cocciutamente convinta della validità delle proprie opinioni, sono pochi gli argomenti che dominano la conversazione dei newyorchesi come quello della casa.

Come qualsiasi altra cosa in questa metropoli, crearsi un accogliente focolare domestico non è cosa facile. Gli appartamenti di New York sono famosi per essere minuscoli, oppure sono così vecchi da richiedere un restauro totale da pavimento a soffitto. Invece di essere scoraggiate da questi ostacoli, orde interminabili di intrepidi proprietari, architetti e progettisti hanno accettato la sfida. Ma in una maestosa metropoli di grattaceli come New York, ristrutturazioni affrettate e arredi tipo Ikea semplicemente non superano l'esame. No, questa città esige appartamenti favolosi, lussuosi e solenni pari alla propria scintillante magnificenza. Le case non devono per forza costare decine di milioni di dollari, ma deve assolutamente sembrare che quello sia il loro valore.

Dalle alte e raffinate villette a schiera di Harlem ai loft assolati della Soho degli artisti, queste lussuose case hanno una loro naturale audacia, sono chic e uniche, delle vere e proprie opere d'arte da museo. E benché questi stravaganti alloggi di New York siano unici come le impronte digitali, hanno in comune un tratto caratteristico: rappresentano il focolare domestico.

Skyline Views

Skying high above the East River in the sumptuously appointed Trump World Tower, this palatial residence provides bird's-eye views of the Empire State and Chrysler buildings, Manhattan and the lands—Long Island, New Jersey—that lay beyond. The apartment's most impressive elements are the floor-to-ceiling windows, through which sun streams and bathes the tastefully modern quarters in a 24-karat golden glow.

Hoch über dem East River befindet sich der luxuriös ausgestattete Trump World Tower. Diese palastartige Wohnung bietet Ausblicke auf das Empire State Buildung und das Chrysler Building, auf Manhattan und die umliegenden Gebiete – Long Island, New Jersey – aus der Vogelperspektive. Die eindrucksvollsten Elemente dieser Wohnung sind jedoch die vom Boden bis zur Decke reichenden Fenster, die Sonne einlassen und diese geschmackvolle, zeitgenössische Wohnung in goldenes Licht tauchen.

La tour Trump World Tower somptueusement aménagée qui se dresse au-dessus de East River est un palace résidentiel qui offre une vue d'ensemble imprenable de l'Empire State building et du Chrysler building, de Manhattan et des bandes de terre qui s'étendent au delà, Long Island et New Jersey. Les éléments les plus marquants de l'appartement sont les fenêtres du sol au plafond à travers lesquels les rayons de soleil inondent ces quartiers modernes et bon goût de leurs reflets dorés.

Questa sontuosa abitazione, che domina l'East River dall'alto del lussuoso edificio Trump World Tower, offre vedute dell'Empire State Buiding e del Chrysler Building, di Manhattan e delle regioni circostanti: Long Island e New Jersey. Gli elementi che colpiscono di più in questo appartamento sono le finestre a tutta parete, attraverso cui passa la luce del sole immergendo le eleganti stanze in uno splendore dorato.

Erigiéndose imponentemente sobre el East River, en la suntuosa "Trump World Tower", esta lujosa residencia ofrece vistas panorámicas de los edificios Empire State y Chrysler, Manhattan, y las tierras aledañas de Long Island y New Jersey. Los elementos más impactantes del piso son sus amplios ventanales que, extendiéndose desde el piso al techo, dejan entrar el sol raudales, transformando sus modernos y elegantes ambientes en una esplendorosa joya de 24 quilates.

Pop Modernist Style

The owners of this two-bedroom, 900-square-foot dwelling ditched its classic look for a showy, contemporary-pop feel. Furthering the theme are oversize orange chairs and an opaque Perspex table. The living room is finished with sliding glass doors that open onto a balcony offering sweeping views of downtown Manhattan. The gleaming kitchen is a contrast of hot and cool, thanks to colored light filters operated by flipping a switch.

Die Eigentümer dieser 80 qm großen Zweizimmerwohnung mit zwei Schlafzimmern haben sich von dem klassischen Look abgewandt und sich statt dessen einem zeitgenössischen Pop-Ambiente verschrieben, das durch riesige orangefarbene Sessel und einen opaken Plexiglas- Tisch verstärkt wird. Vom Wohnzimmer aus gelangt man durch eine gläserne Schiebetür auf einen Balkon, der einen atemberaubenden Blick auf Downtown Manhattan bietet. In der funkelnden Küche kontrastieren warme und kalte Akzente, die durch farbige, durch Schalter bediente Lichtfilter hervorgerufen werden.

Les propriétaires de ce logement de près de 80 m² avec deux chambres ont abandonné son style classique pour un air tape-à-l'œil, pop-contemporain. Pour accentuer le thème, ils ont mis des chaises orange immenses et une table en perspex opaque. Les portes coulissantes en verre qui s'ouvrent sur un balcon offrant une vue panoramique du centre de Manhattan sont la touche spéciales du salon. La cuisine rutilante est un contraste de tons chauds et froids grâce à des lumières filtrées qui s'animent à l'aide d'un interrupteur.

I proprietari di questo appartamento di circa 80 metri quadri, con due camere da letto, hanno deciso di rivoluzionarne l'aspetto classico a favore di un look più contemporaneo e appariscente, stile pop. E per esaltare questa atmosfera pop ci sono enormi poltrone arancioni e un tavolo in perspex opaco. Il soggiorno è completato da porte di vetro scorrevoli che si aprono su un terrazzo che offre ampie vedute del centro di Manhattan. La cucina luccicante è un gioco di toni caldi e freddi, grazie a faretti di luce colorata azionati da un semplice interruttore.

Los propietarios de esta vivienda de 80 metros cuadrados y dos dormitorios, cambiaron su estilo clásico por un diseño pop contemporáneo más llamativo. Realzan esta tendencia las sillas anaranjadas de gran tamaño y una mesa de plexiglás opaco. Completan la decoración de la sala las puertas correderas de vidrio que dan a un balcón con una vista panorámica del centro de Manhattan. La resplandeciente cocina ofrece un contraste de tonos cálidos y fríos, gracias a los filtros de luces de colores que funcionan mediante un interruptor.

MANHATTAN . Pop Modern

Upper East Side Luxury

In the heart of the hectic Big Apple, this sumptuously appointed home serves as a refined, French-flavored refuge. The dining room is a bold combination of vibrant patterns with the floral walls, upholstered in Braquenié linen, offset by a sofa in rose upholstery and a chandelier sprouting dainty daisies. A canopied bed, which is made cozy with a country quilt, dominates the plush, colorful bedroom.

Im Herzen des hektischen Big Apple dient dieses luxuriös ausgestattete Heim als raffinierte Oase der Ruhe im französischen Stil. Im Speisezimmer wurden die verschiedensten ausdrucksvollen Muster verwendet, die Blumentapete aus Leinen wird durch eine roséfarbene Couch und eine Deckenleuchte akzentuiert, aus der Gänseblümchen hervorsprießen. Im farbenfrohen, mit witzigen Designelementen versehenen Schlafzimmer dominiert ein Himmelbett mit einer gemütlichen kuscheligen Steppdecke im Landhausstil.

Au cœur du tourbillon de la Grande Pomme, cette résidence luxueusement aménagée offre un refuge raffiné à la francaise. La salle à manger est un mélange audacieux de couleurs chatoyantes avec des murs tapissés en lin Braquenie aux motifs fleuris qui font jeu au divan tapissé en rose et un lustre agrémenté de marguerites délicates. Un lit à baldaquins devenu douillet avec sa couette campagne, domine une chambre somptueuse et haute en couleurs.

Nel cuore della frenetica Grande Mela, questa lussuosa abitazione offre un raffinato rifugio dal sapore francese. La sala da pranzo è un audace miscuglio di vivaci colori, dove le pareti ricoperte di tessuto Braquenié a fiori si contrappongono alla tappezzeria rosa del divano, il tutto completato da un lampadario composto da preziose margherite. Infine un letto a baldacchino, reso accogliente da una trapunta in stile country, domina la sfarzosa e pittoresca camera da letto.

Enclavada en el corazón de la ajetreada Gran Manzana, esta suntuosa residencia ofrece un refugio elegante, con un acento francés. El comedor es una osada combinación de diseños intensos, en el que el empapelado floral de tela Braquenié se equilibra con el sofá tapizado en rosa y una araña con delicados brotes de margaritas. Una cama con dosel, que se vuelve más acogedora con un edredón estilo country, domina el dormitorio lujoso y colorido.

MANHATTAN . Upper East Side Luxury   37

Former Harlem Church

The former Spanish Harlem house of worship became home to a New York architect and interior designer. Where the church choir once stood now resides the fireplace-equipped bedroom. The lofty, narrow structure possesses numerous arched windows and passageways, which provide both luminosity and beauty, serenity and grace.

Die ehemalige Kirche in Spanish Harlem ist nun das Zuhause eines New Yorker Architekten und Innenausstatters. Das mit einem Kamin ausgestattete Schlafzimmer befindet sich dort, wo einstmals der Chor war. Die Eichenböden wurden gebleicht und weiß gebeizt. Das luftige, schmale Gebäude besitzt zahlreiche Bogenfenster und Durchgänge, die für Helligkeit und Schönheit, Ruhe und Anmut sorgen.

L'ancien lieu de culte espagnol de Harlem est devenu la maison d'un architecte décorateur à New York. Là où se tenait le chœur de l'église, on trouve maintenant la chambre équipée d'une cheminée. La structure étroite de style loft renferme de nombreuses fenêtres avec des voûtes et des corridors qui apporte luminosité, beauté, sérénité et grâce.

Una antigua casa de culto del Spanish Harlem se convirtió en el hogar de un arquitecto y diseñador de interiores de Nueva York. Donde antes estaba el sitio reservado para el coro ahora se erige el dormitorio, equipado con chimenea. La construcción, de techos altos, tiene numerosas ventanas con arco y corredores que le brindan luminosidad y belleza, serenidad y gracia.

Un ex luogo di culto spagnolo di Harlem è stato trasformato nella residenza di un architetto e progettista d'interni newyorkese. Dove un tempo era collocato il coro della chiesa ora si trova la camera da letto allietata da un camino. La struttura, alta e stretta, possiede numerose finestre arcuate e corridoi che le donano sia luminosità che bellezza, sia serenità che leggiadria.

40   MANHATTAN . Former Harlem Church

Sutton Place Penthouse

Clothing designer Lisa Perry turned her 17-room 6,500-square-foot penthouse in Midtown's tony Sutton Place enclave into a Sixties fantasy fit for Warhol and Co. The regal dwelling was stripped of stodgy historical details and decked out with jet-set glamour. Hallway floors gleam with epoxy, and walls are adorned with grand-scale Op and Pop Art works from masters like James Rosenquist, Robert Rauschenberg, Roy Lichtenstein and, of course, Warhol.

Die Modedesignerin Lisa Perry verwandelte ihr Penthouse mit 17 Zimmern und 600 qm am eleganten Sutton Place in eine Fantasie der 1960er Jahre, die Warhol und Co. alle Ehre machen würde. Fade historische Details mussten Jet-Set-Glamour weichen. Die Böden im Flur erhalten ihren Glanz durch Epoxikunstharz und die Wände sind mit großflächigen Op- and Pop-Art-Kunstwerken von Meistern wie James Rosenquist, Robert Rauschenberg, Roy Lichtenstein und natürlich Warhol dekoriert.

Le designer de mode, Lisa Perry a transformé un penthouse de 17 pièces et près de 600 m² dans l'enclave élégante de Sutton Place dans le Midtown en une fantaisie des années 60 digne de Warhol et compagnie. Les accents historiques lourdauds furent enlevés pour être remplacés par du glamour jet-set. Le plancher dans le couloir brille de résine époxy et les murs sont ornés avec des œuvres Op et Pop Art de grande taille, signées par des maitres comme James Rosenquist, Robert Rauschenberg, Roy Lichtenstein et bien sur, Warhol.

La diseñadora de ropa Lisa Perry, convirtió su penthouse de 17 ambientes y 600 metros cuadrados en el distinguido enclave Sutton Place de Midtown en un fantasía de los años sesenta digna de Warhol y su troupe. La majestuosa vivienda fue despojada de sus densos detalles históricos y engalanada con el glamour del jet-set. Los pisos del hall brillan con epoxi y las paredes están adornadas con obras a gran escala del Arte Pop y Op de maestros como James Rosenquist, Robert Rauschenberg, Roy Lichtenstein y, por supuesto, Warhol.

La designer di abbigliamento Lisa Perry ha trasformato i 600 metri quadri del suo attico di 17 stanze che sorge nell'elegante enclave di Sutton Place a Midtown in una fantasia anni sessanta adatta a Warhol e compagnia. La regale abitazione è stata liberata dai dettagli storici che la appesantivano e decorata con il fascino del jet-set. I pavimenti dei corridoi brillano di resina epossidica, e le pareti sono adornate da ampie opere di arte Op e Pop di maestri come James Rosenquist, Robert Rauschenberg, Roy Lichtenstein e, ovviamente, Warhol.

Townhouse Uptown

Movie producer Jenette Kahn gave her Harlem townhouse a total renovation, honoring the past while adding modern touches. A chandelier constructed from paper covered with replicas of Picasso's *Guernica* hangs from the ceiling, near a 1939 Panoram—the world's first video jukebox. Even quirkier are the fireplaces. The dining room's is shaped like a theater stage, and the rear parlor's fireplace tiles mimic book spines. In a study of contrasts, modern art fills a traditional home's nooks and crannies.

Die Filmproduzenten Jenette Kahn hat ihr Townhouse in Harlem total renoviert. Sie behielt alte Elemente bei und fügte moderne Akzente hinzu. Von der Decke hängt ein Kronleuchter aus Papier, der mit Replikaten von Picassos *Guernica* bedeckt ist, neben einem Panoram aus dem Jahr 1939 – der ersten Video-Jukebox der Welt. Die Kamine sind noch schrulliger. Der des Esszimmers hat die Form einer Bühne und die Kacheln um den Kamin im Empfangszimmer sind Buchrücken nachgeahmt. Hier fallen Kontraste ins Auge – moderne Kunst füllt die Ecken und Nischen eines traditionellen Hauses.

La productrice de cinéma Jenette Kahn a complètement rénové sa maison mitoyenne à Harlem, en rendant hommage au passé tout en ajoutant des touches modernes. Un lustre fait de papier couvert de reproductions de *Guernica* de Picasso pend du plafond, près d'un Panoram datant de 1939 – le premier jukebox vidéo. Les cheminées sont encore plus excentriques. La salle à manger a la forme d'une scène de théâtre et les carreaux de la cheminée du boudoir ressemblent à des dos de livres. Dans un style tout en contrastes, l'art moderne remplit les coins et recoins d'une maison traditionnelle.

La productora cinematográfica Jenette Kahn renovó su casa adosada de Harlem en forma total, honrando el pasado pero agregando toques modernos. Del techo pende una araña construida con papel y cubierta con réplicas del *Guernica* de Picasso, cerca de una Panoram 1939, la primera video rocola del mundo. Aún más singulares son las chimeneas. El comedor tiene la forma de un escenario y mientras que las de la chimenea de la sala trasera semejan el lomo de un libro. En un estudio de contrastes, cada rincón de este hogar tradicional está lleno de arte moderno.

La produttrice cinematografica Jenette Kahn ha completamente ristrutturato la sua villetta di Harlem, rendendo omaggio al passato ma anche aggiungendo dei tocchi di modernità. Un lampadario costruito con carte rappresentanti repliche della *Guernica* di Picasso pende dal soffitto, vicino ad un Panoram del 1939 – il primo jukebox al mondo di video. Ancora più particolari sono i camini. Quello della sala da pranzo ha l'aspetto di un palcoscenico teatrale; le mattonelle di quello del salottino posteriore assomigliano a coste di libri. Alla ricerca di contrasto, l'arte moderna riempie ogni angolo e ogni fenditura di una casa tradizionale.

MANHATTAN . Townhouse Uptown

GOLDEN YELLA GIRL

Tiny Space

Despite dwelling in a 300-square-foot Upper East Side studio containing a single closet, designer Giuseppe Pica dreamed big. His tromp-l'oeil techniques included laying down beige carpet and painting most surfaces white, cabinets included. From this blank palette, Pica built "separate" rooms: The living area is defined by a sheepskin rug, a small coffee table topped with geometric shapes, and plush tufted chairs that recall deflated toadstools.

Der Designer Giuseppe Pica hatte große Träume, obwohl er in einem nicht einmal 30 qm großen Einzimmerapartment mit nur einem Einbauschrank an der Upper East Side wohnt. Zu seinen Tromp-l'Oeil-Techniken gehörte, dass er einen beigefarbenen Teppich verlegte und alle Flächen, einschließlich fast aller Schränke, weiß strich. Er benutzte diese uniforme Palette, um „separate" Zimmer zu bauen: Der Wohnraum wird durch einen Teppich aus Schaffell, einen kleinen geometrischen Couchtisch und plüschige Sessel, die an formlose Pilze erinnern, abgegrenzt.

Bien qu'il habite dans moins de 30 m², le dessinateur Giuseppe Pica a eu une vision grandiose pour son studio dans l'Upper East Side studio qui ne contient qu'un seul placard. Ses techniques en trompe-l'œil ont consisté à mettre de la moquette beige et à peindre la plupart des surfaces en blanc, y compris les placards muraux. A partir de cette palette, Pica a construit des pièces « séparées » : le séjour est défini par un tapi en peau de mouton, une petite table basse avec un dessus souligné par des formes géométriques et des fauteuils moelleux qui rappellent des champignons désenflés.

El hecho de vivir en un estudio de 27 metros cuadrados, con un solo placard, en el Upper East Side, no le impidió al diseñador Giuseppe Pica soñar a lo grande. Sus técnicas tromp-l'oeil consistieron en colocar alfombras color beige y pintar la mayoría de las superficies de color blanco, hasta los armarios. Partiendo de esta gama lisa, Pica construyó habitaciones "separadas": al sector del living lo definen una alfombra de piel de cordero, una pequeña mesa de café sobre la que se colocaron formas geométricas y sillas almohadilladas de felpa que parecen hongos achatados.

Pur abitando in un monolocale di 27 metri quadri nell'Upper East Side contenente un singolo armadio a muro, il progettista d'interni Giuseppe Pica ha sognato in grande. Tra le sue tecniche tromp-l'oeil figurano l'aver scelto una moquette beige e l'aver dipinto quasi tutte le superfici, comprese le credenze, di bianco. Da questa tavolozza di bianchi, Pica ha creato stanze "separate": la zona salotto è definita da un tappeto di pelle di pecora, un piccolo tavolino ricoperto di forme geometriche e soffici sedie a pelo lungo che ricordano dei funghi a cappello sgonfi.

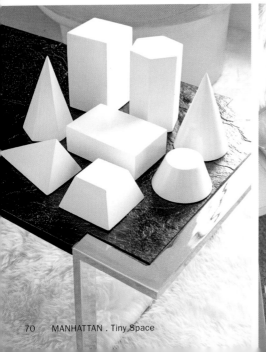

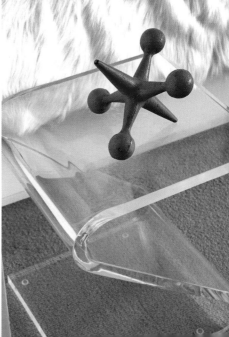

Harlem Grandeur

Interior designers Robert F. Wagner and Timothy Van Dam painstakingly restored this nineteenth-century Harlem townhouse to its freshly built glamour and filled it with carefully sourced antique furnishings. The deep-red dining room is decked out with a drooping, glittering chandelier, 1920s Far East carpet and Federal-era chairs from 1820.

Innenarchitekten Robert F. Wagner und Timothy Van Dam haben dieses Townhouse im Stadtteil Harlem aus dem 19. Jahrhundert minutiös renoviert, so dass der Glanz vergangener Zeiten wiederhergestellt und das Haus mit umsichtig ausgewählten Antiquitäten ausgestattet wurde. Das Speisezimmer ist in einem satten Rot gehalten und mit einem funkelnden Kronleuchter dekoriert sowie einem Teppich aus dem Fernen Osten, der aus den 1920er Jahren stammt, und klassizistischen Stühlen aus den USA aus der Zeit um 1820.

Décorateurs Robert F. Wagner et Timothy Van Dam ont restauré minutieusement cette maison mitoyenne du XIXe à Harlem pour lui donner son glamour de nouvelle construction remplie de pièces d'antiquité triées sur le volet. La salle à manger rouge de Chine est agrémentée d'un lustre scintillant qui pend du plafond, le tapis Extrême-Orient des années 1920 et les fauteuils de l'époque fédérale qui datent de 1820.

Diseñadores de interiores Robert F. Wagner y Timothy Van Dam restauraron en detalle esta casa adosada del siglo diecinueve en Harlem para darle este fresco glamour y hacerla albergar un mobiliario antiguo cuidadosamente seleccionado. El comedor de un color rojo intenso está engalanado con una fastuosa y lánguida araña, una alfombra de los años veinte del Extremo Oriente y sillas de 1820 del período Federal.

Progettisti d'interni Robert F. Wagner e Timothy Van Dam hanno meticolosamente ristrutturato questo villino a schiera di Harlem del diciannovesimo secolo, riportandolo al suo fascino originario e riempiendolo di arredi antichi scelti con cura. La sala da pranzo di un rosso scuro è decorata con uno scintillante lampadario pendente, con un tappeto dell'estremo oriente degli anni '20 e con sedie stile periodo federale del 1820.

Harlem Home Office

When milliner Rod Keenan bought his four-story, Queen Anne-style Harlem townhouse, it was but a shell. Now it's a lovely, live-work hybrid: Keenan's workroom is filled with wooden blocks for shaping hats and brims, sewing machines and the odd globe. Residing in his building are two equally creative tenants, makeup artist Frankie Boyd and style writer Cator Sparks, whose home office reflects the artistic live-work atmosphere.

Als der Modist Rod Keenan sein viergeschossiges Townhouse in Harlem im Queen Anne-Stil kaufte, war es lediglich ein Gerippe. Nun ist es ein zauberhafter Mehrzweckbau: Der Arbeitsraum von Keanan ist mit Holzblöcken vollgestellt, die er zum Formen von Hüten und Huträndern verwendet, sowie Nähmaschinen und dem hier fremd anmutenden Globus. Die beiden Mieter, die in diesem Gebäude leben, sind ebenso kreativ. Es handelt sich um den Make-up Artist Frankie Boyd und den Style Writer Cator Sparks, in dessen Home Office sich die Atmosphäre eines künstlerischen Wohn- und Arbeitsplatzes wiederspiegelt.

Lorsque le modiste Rod Keenan fit l'acquisition de sa maison mitoyenne de quatre étages style Reine Anne dans Harlem, ce n'était rien d'autre qu'une carcasse. Mais maintenant c'est un charmant duo travail et demeure : l'espace travail de Keenan est remplie de pièces de bois pour modeler les chapeaux et les bords, machines à coudre et un globe inattendu. Deux locataires tout aussi créatifs résident dans son immeuble, le maquilleur Frankie Boyd et l'écrivain de style Cator Sparks, dont le bureau à la maison reflète l'atmosphère artistique maison et lieu de travail.

Cuando el fabricante de sombreros Rod Keenan la compró, la casa adosada (townhouse) de cuatro pisos de estilo reina Ana en Harlem no era más que una estructura. Hoy es un bello híbrido vivienda-trabajo: la sala de trabajo de Keenan está llena de bloques de madera para modelar sombreros y alas, máquinas de coser y una lámpara. En su edificio viven dos inquilinos igualmente creativos, el artista del maquillaje Frankie Boyd y Cator Sparks, quien escribe sobre moda y cuya vivienda-oficina refleja la atmósfera artística de esa dualidad casa-trabajo.

Quando il modista Rod Keenan acquistò ad Harlem il suo villino a quattro piani in stile Regina Anna, esso non era altro che un guscio. Ora è un adorabile ibrido casa-lavoro: il laboratorio di Keenan è pieno dei blocchi in legno che egli usa per dare la forma a cappelli e falde, di macchine da cucire e di un insolito globo. Nel suo edificio risiedono due inquilini altrettanto creativi, l'artista del trucco Frankie Boyd e lo scrittore di moda Cator Sparks, il cui ufficio in casa riflette l'atmosfera casa-lavoro degli artisti; la sua scrivania antica è circondata da cornici che racchiudono fotografie e illustrazioni ispiratrici.

Uptown Residence

Artist Ursula Hodel's Upper East Side aerie, perched high above the naturalistic sweeps of Central Park, is loaded to the gills with eye-jolting artwork that demands your attention and give each room an idiosyncratic flavor. Fun, jazzy flair suffuses the living room, with the kinetic black-and-white paintings joined by the geometric rug and lustrous, coal-hued piano.

Das Penthouse der Künstlerin Ursula Hodel an der Upper East Side hoch über der Baumlandschaft des Central Park ist voller atemberaubender Kunstwerke, die die Aufmerksamkeit auf sich ziehen und jedem Raum eine spezifische Note verleihen. Im Wohnzimmer lassen die kinetischen, schwarz-weißen Gemälde, die mit dem geometrischen Teppich und den glänzenden, anthrazitfarbenen Flügel eine Einheit bilden, an Jazz und Lebensfreude denken.

Le nid d'aigle de l'artiste Ursula Hodel dans l'Upper East Side perché très haut au-dessus des étendues verdoyantes de Central Park, est rempli d'œuvres d'art qui vous sautent aux yeux et donnent à chaque pièce un ton bien particulier. Une atmosphère gaie, très jazz infuse le séjour avec des tableaux cinétiques noirs et blancs qui font jeu avec le tapis géométrique et un piano lustré avec des tons anthracite.

La atalaya del artista Ursula Hodel, enclavada en lo alto de la extensa naturaleza del Central Park, está cargada de obras de arte asombrosas que llaman la atención y le dan a cada habitación un sabor característico. Un estilo alegre y llamativo envuelve la sala donde las cinéticas pinturas en blanco y negro se unen a las geométricas alfombras y al lustroso piano con tonos de color carbón.

L'inaccessibile rifugio dell'artista Ursula Hodel nell'Upper East Side, da cui si dominano le ampie distese naturalistiche di Central Park, è strapieno di appariscenti opere d'arte che richiamano l'attenzione e che donano ad ogni stanza una fragranza particolarissima. Un'aria divertente e briosa si cosparge sul salotto, con i dinamici quadri in bianco e nero che richiamano il tappeto dai disegni geometrici ed il lucente pianoforte color carbone.

Upper West Side Exotic

In the Upper West Side's landmark Beaux-Arts building Ansonia, jewelry designer John Hardy and wife Cynthia have transformed their apartment into an Indonesian-inspired refuge. Hardy designed most of the exotic furniture and fixtures himself, from the angular chairs hammered construction from palmwood and leather to the rustic wood dining table abutting Hardy's photograph of a Balinese volcano. A touch of Indonesia in the heart of Manhattan.

Der Schmuckdesigner John Hardy und seine Frau Cynthia haben ihr Apartment in dem bekannten Beaux-Arts-Gebäude Ansonia an der Upper West Side in eine Oase mit indonesischem Flair verwandelt. Die meisten exotischen Möbel und Lampen hat Hardy selbst entworfen, angefangen bei den kantigen Stühlen aus Palmenholz und Leder bis zu dem rustikalen Esstisch neben Hardys Foto eines Vulkans auf Bali. Ein Hauch Indonesien im Herzen Manhattans.

Dans l'immeuble d'Ansonia qui est le symbole des beaux-arts dans le Upper West Side, le joailler John Hardy et sa femme Cynthia ont transformé leur appartement en un refuge de style indonésien. Hardy a conçu la majeure partie des meubles et des finitions exotiques lui-même, des fauteuils angulaires martelés en bois de palme et cuir à la table rustique en bois contenant la photo de Hardy d'un volcan à Bali. Une touche d'Indonésie en plein cœur de Manhattan.

En el famoso edificio Ansonia de estilo Beaux Arts en el Upper West Side, el diseñador de joyas John Hardy y su esposa Cynthia transformaron su apartamento en un refugio inspirado en Indonesia. Fue el mismo Hardy quien diseñó la mayoría del exótico mobiliario y las instalaciones, desde las angulosas sillas construidas con madera de palma y cuero hasta la mesa del comedor de madera rústica junto a la cual hay una fotografía tomada por Hardy de un volcán de Bali. Una pincelada de Indonesia en el corazón de Manhattan.

Nello splendido edificio Ansonia in stile Beaux-Arts dell'Upper West Side, il gioielliere stilista John Hardy e la moglie Cynthia hanno trasformato il loro appartamento in un rifugio di ispirazione indonesiana. Hardy ha progettato la maggior parte delle suppellettili e degli arredi esotici, dalle sedie angolari martellate costruite in legno di palma e pelle, al rustico tavolo da pranzo in legno a ridosso della fotografia di Hardy di un vulcano balinese. Un pizzico di Indonesia nel cuore di Manhattan.

Sumptuous Uptown

Situated in a modern Upper East Side tower overlooking the East River, Naomi and André Altholz's elegantly funky apartment was dressed by legendary interior designer Carlo Rampazzi. In the living room, a super-soft fox-fur chair is matched to whimsical touches like the turtle sculpture, which guests can sit on. Lastly, the couple's daughter's bedroom is an electric mix of colors that look as scrumptious as candy.

Das elegant-unkonventionelle Apartment von Naomi and André Altholz in einem Wolkenkratzer an der Upper East Side wurde von dem legendären Innenarchitekten Carlo Rampazzi ausgestattet. Im Wohnraum sind ein superweicher Sessel aus Kunstpelz und witzige Elemente aufeinander abgestimmt, wie die Skulptur einer Schildkröte, die Gäste als Sitzgelegenheit benutzen können. Das Schlafzimmer der Tochter des Hauses ist eine elektrifizierende Farbmischung, die so lecker aussieht wie Bonbons.

Situé dans une tour moderne donnant sur la rivière est dans l'Upper East Side, l'appartement élégant et funky de Naomi et André Altholz est signé par le célèbre décorateur légendaire, Carlo Rampazzi. Dans le salon, un fauteuil super doux en fourrure de renard est assorti à des éléments fantasques comme une sculpture de tortue sur laquelle les invités peuvent s'assoir. Enfin, la chambre de la fille du couple est un ensemble éclectique de couleurs qui rappellent des bonbons délicieux.

Ubicado en una moderna torre del Upper East Side con vista al East River, el apartamento de Naomi y André Altholz, que despliega una elegancia original, fue decorado por el legendario diseñador de interiores Carlo Rampazzi. En la sala, una silla tapizada con una piel de zorro muy suave armoniza con toques fantásticos como la escultura de una tortuga, sobre la que los invitados pueden sentarse. Por último, el dormitorio de la hija de la pareja es una combinación ecléctica de colores que resulta tan tentadora como un dulce.

Situato in un moderno edificio a torre dell'Upper East Side che si affaccia sull'East River, l'appartamento di Naomi e André Altholz, funky ed elegante, è stato progettato dal leggendario architetto d'interni Carlo Rampazzi. Nel salotto, una sedia supermorbida di pelliccia di volpe è abbinata a tocchi stravaganti come la scultura di una tartaruga su cui possono accomodarsi gli ospiti. Infine, la camera da letto della figlia è una combinazione elettrica di colori che appaiono gustosi come caramelle.

Upper East Side Elegance

Timeless, old-New York sophistication pervades this Upper East Side residence dripping with bewitching details. The library is anointed with handsome wooden bookshelves, curved moldings integrated with columns and an attractive wooden desk paired with richly upholstered chairs. The grand living room's floor-dwarfing rug, flower paintings and sumptuous couches are enlivened with Far East-style chests, while a jet-black piano holds court near the windows.

In diesem Heim an der Upper East Side herrscht die zeitlose Eleganz alteingesessener New Yorker mit zahllosen bezaubernden Details vor. Die Bibliothek ist mit schönen, hölzernen Bücherregalen ausgestattet, gekehlte Zierleisten werden von Säulen unterbrochen und um den attraktiven Holzschreibtisch befinden sich üppige Polstersessel. Der riesige Teppich, die Blumengemälde und die luxuriösen Couchen werden durch Kommoden im fernöstlichen Stil akzentuiert, während ein pechschwarzer Flügel in der Nähe der Fenster Hof hält. Im Speisebereich befinden sich ein geschwungener Tisch und ein Kronleuchter.

La sophistication éternelle du New York d'époque imprègne cette résidence dans l'Upper East Side avec une abondance d'accents ensorcelants. La bibliothèque est parée de beaux rayons en bois, des moulures arrondies qui s'intègrent aux colonnes et un charmant bureau en bois assorti aux chaises richement tapissés. Le grand séjour a un immense tapis, des tableaux de fleurs et des divans somptueux rehaussés avec des commodes de style Extrême-Orient et un piano d'un noir de jais qui trône près des fenêtres. L'espace salle à manger est agrémenté d'une banquette recourbée et d'un lustre suspendu.

La eterna sofisticación de la antigua Nueva York reina en esta residencia de Upper East Side llena de cautivantes detalles. La biblioteca está coronada con elegantes estantes de madera, molduras curvas integradas con columnas y un atractivo escritorio de madera que hace juego con sillas suntuosamente tapizadas. La impresionante alfombra del living, las pinturas con motivos florales y los espléndidos sofás están complementados con arcones del estilo Extremo Oriente, mientras un piano negro azabache ubicado cerca de las ventanas es el centro de la atención. La zona del comedor ostenta un banco curvo y una araña de caireles.

Senza tempo, antica – la ricercatezza di New York permea questa dimora dell'Upper East Side da cui trapelano dettagli affascinanti. La biblioteca è santificata da una splendida libreria in legno, una cornice ricurva integrata a colonne e un'elegante scrivania affiancata da sedie dalla ricca tappezzeria. L'immenso tappeto del maestoso salotto, i quadri con motivi floreali e i sontuosi divani sono rallegrati da credenze in stile orientale e da un pianoforte nero corvino che regna accanto alle finestre. La zona pranzo è allestita con una panca con schienale imbottito e un lampadario a gocce.

Upper East Side Vintage

Fashion plate Tiffany Dubin's fascination with vintage garb led her to convert her Upper East Side apartment into a glorious mish-mash of twentieth-century classics, flea-market finds and eclectic, colorful kitsch. The living room is loaded with '60s and '70s furniture, art objects and provocative, fashion-themed artwork.

Die Faszination der Modediva Tiffany Dubin für Kleider aus vergangenen Zeiten veranlasste sie dazu, ihr Apartment an New Yorks Upper East Side in eine kunstvolle Mischung aus Klassikern des 20. Jahrhunderts, Fundstücken von Flohmärkten und eklektischem, farbenfrohem Kitsch zu verwandeln. An Kunstobjekten und provokativen Kunstwerken zum Thema Mode vorbei gelangt man in den Wohnraum, der mit Möbeln aus den 60er und 70er Jahren bestückt ist.

La passion de Tiffany Dubin, une vraie gravure de mode, pour les habits vintage l'a amené à transformer son appartement dans l'Upper East Side en un fantastique méli-mélo de classiques du vingtième siècle avec des trouvailles éclectiques dénichées dans des brocantes et du kitsch chatoyant. Des objets d'art et des œuvres provocantes avec un thème de mode qui mènent à dans la salle de séjour rempli de meubles des années 60 et 70.

Su fascinación por los atuendos de época llevó a Tiffany Dubin, un símbolo de la moda, a convertir su apartamento del Upper East Side en una soberbia mezcla de clásicos del siglo XX, adquisiciones de los mercados de pulgas y eclécticos y coloridos elementos kitsch. Piezas y provocativas obras con temas de moda conducen hacia la sala cargada de mobiliario de los años 60 y 70.

Il fascino esercitato dall'abbigliamento d'epoca sulla splendida Tiffany Dubin, la ha sospinta a convertire il suo appartamento nell'Upper East Side in una magnifica accozzaglia di classici del ventesimo secolo, di tesori rinvenuti in mercatini delle pulci e di eclettici e variopinti fronzoli kitsch. Vi accompagnano in salotto, traboccante di mobili anni '60 e '70, degli oggetti artistici e dei provocanti capolavori in tema di moda.

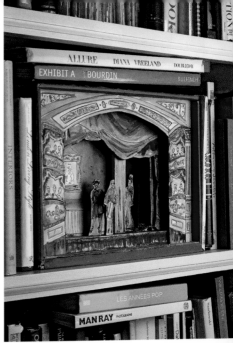

Garment District Loft

Situated in the century-old headquarters of a publishing company in NYC's Garment District, chocolatier Bruce Gilardi's 1,800-square-foot loft is brilliantly lit on even the cloudiest afternoon. The open layout creates little privacy—even the elevated bathtub, surrounded by several of Gilardi's turn-of-the-century Swiss posters, lacks a curtain. Nonetheless, walls' absence gives the apartment a grand spaciousness, and Gilardi has smartly created independent elements.

Das ca. 170 qm große Loft des Chocolatiers Bruce Gilardi befindet sich in der mehr als 100 Jahre alten Zentrale eines Verlags im Garment District von New York City. Selbst bei trübstem Wetter sind die Lichtverhältnisse in dem Loft hervorragend. Der offene Grundriss bietet nur wenig Privatsphäre – sogar die erhöhte Badewanne, die von mehreren Schweizer Jahrhundertwende-Postern umgeben ist, hat keinen Vorhang. Die fehlenden Wände verleihen dem Apartment eine grandiose Weiträumigkeit und Gilardi hat sehr clever unabhängige Elemente geschaffen.

Située dans les bureaux datant d'un siècle d'une société d'édition dans le quartier de la confection de New York, le loft d'environ 170 m² du chocolatier Bruce Gilardi est brillamment éclairé même pendant les après-midis les plus brumeux. L'espace ouvert ne favorise guère l'intimité, même la baignoire surélevée et entourée de posters suisses de Giraldi datant de la fin du siècle dernier, n'a pas de rideau. Mais l'absence de murs rend cet appartement extrêmement spacieux et Gilardi a astucieusement créé des éléments indépendants.

Situado en las centenarias oficinas de una compañía editora en el Garment District de Nueva York, el loft de casi 170 metros cuadrados de Bruce Gilardi, el empresario de los chocolates, está lleno de luz aun en las tardes más nubladas. El gran espacio abierto permite poca privacidad. Encima del nivel del piso y rodeada de varios de los pósteres suizos de fines de siglo que posee Gilardi está la bañera, sin cortinas. Sin embargo, la ausencia de paredes le da al apartamento una gran amplitud, y Gilardi ha creado con ingenio elementos independientes.

Ubicati nella sede centenaria di una società editrice nel Garment District di New York, i 170 metri quadri del loft del produttore di cioccolata Bruce Gilardi sono luminosissimi anche nei pomeriggi più nuvolosi. La pianta aperta crea poca privacy – nemmeno la vasca da bagno rialzata, circondata da vari poster svizzeri di inizio secolo del Gilardi, ha una tenda. Ma se l'assenza di pareti dona all'appartamento spaziosità, Gilardi ha abilmente creato zone indipendenti.

MANHATTAN Garment District 2002 129

Gramercy Park Treasure

A lifelong collector's passion for art that's by turns eclectic, historic and iconic is displayed in his gracious duplex apartment overlooking Manhattan's bucolic Gramercy Park. The dwelling is decorated with artwork encompassing a diverse mash-up of civilizations and cultures. In the living room, Far Eastern works are juxtaposed with modernistic pieces.

In diesem einladenden, zweigeschossigen Apartment am idyllischen Gramercy Park in Manhattan sind die eklektischen, historischen und ikonischen Kunstgegenstände dieses lebenslangen Sammlers zu bewundern. Die Wohnung ist mit Kunstwerken aus den unterschiedlichsten Zivilisationen und Kulturen dekoriert. Im Wohnraum bilden Arbeiten aus dem Fernen Osten und modernistische Stücke gekonnte Gegensätze.

Une passion pour les arts à la fois éclectiques, historiques et iconiques toute une vie durant, se manifeste dans cet appartement duplex gracieux qui donne sur le Parc bucolique de Gramercy dans Manhattan. La demeure est décorée avec des œuvres d'art qui représentent un brassage incroyable de civilisations et cultures. Dans le séjour, des œuvres d'Extrême-Orient se juxtaposent avec des pièces modernistes.

La eterna pasión de un coleccionista por formas de arte a veces eclécticas, a veces históricas, y otras veces icónicas, se despliega en su refinado dúplex que mira al bucólico Gramercy Park de Manhattan. La vivienda está decorada con obras de arte que abarcan una variada gama de civilizaciones y culturas. En la sala, obras del Extremo Oriente se yuxtaponen con obras modernas.

La passione per l'arte che da una vita arde nell'animo di questo collezionista, e che a volte ha assunto caratteri eclettici, a volte storici e a volte iconografici, viene messa in mostra nel suo elegante appartamento su due piani che si affaccia sul bucolico Gramercy Park di Manhattan. L'abitazione è decorata con delle opere d'arte che abbracciano una grande varietà di civiltà e culture. Nel salotto, opere dell'estremo oriente sono giustapposte a pezzi moderni.

Downtown Loft

From circa-1880s denture factory to dream home: Architect David Ling converted a red-brick industrial brownstone in downtown Manhattan into a live-work loft that's a balance of new and old, city and nature. Skylights surrounded by rusting metal beams bring in ample sunlight, illuminating a silver plastic floor and a man-made moat.

Vom Dentallabor von um 1880 zum heutigen Traumhaus: Der Architekt David Ling hat ein Gewerbegebäude aus rotem Ziegel in Downtown Manhattan in ein Loft verwandelt, das sein Lebenswerk ist. Neu und Alt, Stadt und Natur halten sich hier die Waage. Durch die von rostigen Metallbalken umgebenen Oberlichter fällt das Sonnenlicht auf einen silberfarbenen Kunststoffboden und einen Wassergraben.

Transformation spectaculaire d'une usine de dentiers datant d'environ 1880 en une maison de rêve : l'architecte David Ling a converti un bâtiment industriel en briques de grès rouge dans le centre de Manhattan en un loft habitable qui allie parfaitement le nouveau et l'ancien, la ville et la nature. Les lucarnes entourées de poutres de métal rouillé font entrer la lumière du jour en abondance pour illuminer un sol avec revêtement plastifié argent et une douve faite sur mesure.

De un laboratorio dental de la década de 1880 al hogar soñado: el arquitecto David Ling transformó un brownstone industrial de ladrillos rojos en el centro de Manhattan en un loft para vivienda y trabajo que constituye un equilibrio entre lo nuevo y lo viejo, entre la ciudad y la naturaleza. Las claraboyas enmarcadas por vigas de metal oxidado aportan abundante luz que ilumina un piso plástico plateado y un foso.

Da fabbrica di dentiere (1880 circa) a casa dei sogni: l'architetto David Ling ha convertito un edificio industriale in arenaria rossa al centro storico di Manhattan in un loft dove vivere e lavorare, che rappresenta uno squisito equilibrio di nuovo e vecchio, di città e natura. Lucernari circondati da travi di metallo arrugginito consentono alla luce di entrare in abbondanza, illuminando un pavimento in plastica argentata e un fossato appositamente creato.

Downtown Residence

The dwelling's cramped layout is no hindrance to creating distinct rooms: An angled wall divider separates the bedroom. On the divider's other side, the little living room feels grander, owing to eccentric, eye-catching touches such as an electric-blue coffee table crowned with a toy bus and a hand sculpture.

Trotz des geringen Platzes wurden in diesem Apartment deutlich abgegrenzte Räume geschaffen: Das Schlafzimmer wird durch einen über Eck verlaufenden Raumtrenner abgeteilt. Auf der anderen Seite des Raumtrenners erhält das kleine Wohnzimmer durch exzentrische, ins Auge fallende Akzente, wie einen Couchtisch in intensivem Blau, auf dem ein Spielzeugbus und die Skulptur einer Hand steht, mehr Geräumigkeit.

La disposition exiguë du logement n'empêche pas d'obtenir des pièces séparées : un meuble d'angle crée une séparation pour la chambre. De l'autre coté du meuble d'angle, le petit séjour parait plus ample en raison de touches excentriques qui attirent le regard comme une table basse d'un bleu électrique sur laquelle sont posés un bus miniature et la sculpture d'une main.

La reducida superficie de la vivienda no representa un obstáculo para crear habitaciones bien diferenciadas: una mampara angular separa la habitación de la pequeña sala que parece más grande debido a toques excéntricos y llamativos como una mesa de café de un azul eléctrico sobre la que se luce un autobús de juguete, y la escultura de una mano.

Le ristrette dimensioni di questo appartamento non impediscono che vi si creino stanze separate: una parete divisoria ad angolo retto separa la camera da letto. Dall'altro lato del divisorio, il salotto, nonostante le sue dimensioni limitate, sembra molto più ampio grazie ad elementi eccentrici ed appariscenti come un tavolino blu elettrico su cui si ergono un autobus giocattolo e la scultura di una mano.

Soho Loft

Gallerist Sean Kelly and wife Mary's Soho loft serves as an extension and celebration of their artistic passion, with paintings, photographs and works of art filling their capacious, open-layout living quarters lined with blond wooden floors. Exposed wood beams and aged metal poles symbolically separate the dining area from the bordering living room, where conversations are facilitated by an array of couches, shapely chairs and stools surrounding a colossal square coffee table.

Im Loft des Galeristen Sean Kelly und seiner Frau Mary im Stadtteil Soho kommt deren künstlerische Leidenschaft durch Gemälde, Fotografien und Kunstwerke zum Ausdruck, die ihren weitläufigen Wohnbereich mit offenem Grundriss und goldbraunen Holzböden füllen. Der Essbereich wird vom angrenzenden Wohnbereich durch freigelegte Holzbalken und brünierte Metallstangen symbolisch abgetrennt. Im Wohnbereich bieten verschiedene Couchen, ansprechend geformte Sessel und Hocker, die um einen riesigen Couchtisch angeordnet sind, ausreichend Gelegenheiten für Gespräche.

Le loft de Soho des propriétaire de galerie, Sean Kelly et sa femme est comme un prolongement et une célébration de leur passion pour les arts, avec des tableaux, des photos et des œuvres d'art qui remplissent leur vaste espace de conception ouverte souligné par un plancher de bois blond. Des poutres en bois au plafond et des poteaux anciens en métal séparent symboliquement l'espace salle à manger du séjour adjacent propice aux conversations avec toute une batterie de canapés, fauteuils confortables et sièges entourant une table basse carrée et gigantesque.

El loft en el Soho del galerista Sean Kelly y su esposa Mary constituye una continuidad de su pasión artística y un festejo. Esto se ve en las pinturas, fotografías y piezas de arte que llenan el living de diseño abierto y espacioso enmarcado en pisos de madera clara. El sector del comedor está separado simbólicamente con vigas de madera a la vista y postes de metal del lindante living que se presta a las charlas en un despliegue de sofás, hermosas sillas y taburetes ubicados alrededor de una colosal mesa de centro cuadrada.

Il loft di Soho del gallerista Sean Kelly e di sua moglie Mary funge da estensione e celebrazione della loro passione artistica, con dipinti, fotografie e opere d'arte che riempiono lo spazioso ambiente a pianta aperta, messo in risalto da pavimenti di legno biondo. Travi esposte in legno e vecchi pali di metallo separano simbolicamente la zona pranzo dal vicino salotto, dove la conversazione è favorita da una serie di divani, sedie armoniose e sgabelli tutti sistemati attorno ad un colossale tavolino quadrato.

Soho Minimalist

Performance artist Marina Abramović's sun-soaked dwelling (located in an artists-only cooperative building that once housed manufacturing firms) is dotted with columns and sparsely decorated, with the radiant milky ceilings unblemished by artwork. Instead, Abramović prefers strategically placed color blasts, such as the lavender sectional couch and topping her headboard-backed bed with vivid linens.

In dem spärlich dekorierten, sonnendurchfluteten Apartment der Performancekünstlerin Marina Abramović werden durch einzelne Säulen Akzente gesetzt. Es befindet sich in einem Künstlern vorbehaltenen Coop-Gebäude, in dem früher Fertigungsbetriebe untergebracht waren. Die leuchtenden milchigen Decken sind frei von Kunstwerken. Stattdessen bevorzugt Abramović strategisch eingesetzte Farbtupfer, wie die lavendelfarbene Couch oder leuchtende Bettwäsche auf ihrem mit Kopfteil versehenem Bett.

Le logement inondé de soleil de l'artiste Marina Abramović (qui se trouve dans un immeuble coopératif, réservé uniquement aux artistes et abritait jadis des manufactures) est paré de colonnes et décoré sobrement avec des plafonds brillants d'un blanc laiteux et sans aucun ornement. Abramović préfère des touches de couleur éclatante dans des endroits stratégiques comme le canapé d'angle mauve et une literie de couleur vive qui fait jeu avec une grande tête de lit.

La luminosa vivienda de la artista Marina Abramović (ubicada en un edificio de apartamentos cooperativos solo para artistas, que anteriormente estuvo ocupado por empresas manufactureras) está enmarcada por columnas y escasamente decorada. Los techos, de un blanco radiante, no muestran rastros de obras de arte. En cambio, Abramović prefiere oleadas de color estratégicamente ubicadas: el sofá de módulos color lavanda y la cama con respaldo vestida con colores vívidos.

L'appartamento assolato dell'artista performer Marina Abramović (situato in un edificio-cooperativa per soli artisti che un tempo ospitava aziende manifatturiere) è punteggiato da colonne, caratterizzato da una decorazione rada, con luminosi soffitti bianco-latte e incontaminato da opere d'arte. Invece, l'Abramović preferisce esplosioni di colore strategicamente collocate, come il divano modulare color lavanda e il letto con testiera ricoperto di biancheria dai colori intensi.

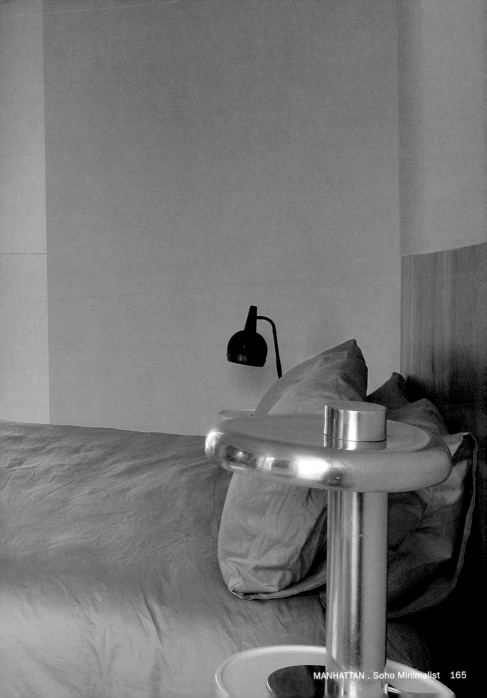

Mid-Century Dwelling

Furniture collector and dealer Matt Damon has turned his apartment into a highly functional living museum dedicated to mid-century modern masterpieces. The well-apportioned dining room is decked out with artist Paul Evans' bronze table and chairs, steel and gold-brazed cabinets, sculpted-steel pole lamp and a room grill designed to look like fish scales.

Der Möbelsammler und -händler Matt Damon hat sein Apartment in ein hochfunktionales, lebendes Museum verwandelt, das modernen Meisterstücken aus der Mitte des Jahrhunderts gewidmet ist. In dem ausgewogen ausgestatteten Speisezimmer befindet sich ein Bronzetisch und Stühle des Künstlers Paul Evans, Schränke aus Stahl mit Goldeinfassungen, eine künstlerisch gestaltete Stehlampe aus Stahl und ein Gitter mit Fischschuppenmuster.

Collectionneur et vendeur de meubles, Matt Damon a transformé son appartement en un musée hautement fonctionnel consacré aux œuvres d'art modernes des années 1950. La salle à manger bien proportionnée est décorée par une table et des chaises en bronze de l'artiste Paul Evans, des placards de rangement en acier et dorures, un lampadaire en acier sculpté et un grill d'intérieur conçu pour donner l'apparence d'écailles de poisson.

El coleccionista de muebles y anticuario Matt Damon ha convertido su apartamento en un muy funcional museo habitado y dedicado a obras maestras del arte de la posguerra. El bien proporcionado comedor está decorado con mobiliario del artista Paul Evans: mesa y sillas de bronce, vitrinas de acero con soldaduras de oro, una lámpara de pie esculpida en acero y un grill con apariencia de escamas de pez.

Matt Damon, collezionista e commerciante di mobili, ha convertito il suo appartamento in un museo vivente estremamente funzionale, dedicato ad opere moderne di metà '900. La sala da pranzo, ben distribuita, è ornata con tavolo e sedie in bronzo dell'artista Paul Evans, armadietti in acciaio e oro brasato, una lampada a palo in acciaio scolpito e una grata progettata per assomigliare a scaglie di pesce.

Chelsea Apartment

A genteel air pervades this gentlemanly dwelling. It features an all-in-one living, kitchen and dining room decorated with a mix of museum-worthy relics and groovy elements like cast-bronze lamps. Instead of consuming precious square feet, the kitchen maximizes the minimal space. Instead of overwhelming the apartment with art, the owner displays several tasteful, conversation-starting selections.

In dieser Wohnung verspürt man eine vornehme Aura. Wohnzimmer, Küche und Esszimmer befinden tsich in einem Raum, in dem eine Mischung aus Stücken von Museumsqualität und ausgefallenen Elemente, wie die aus Bronze gegossenen Lampen zu bewundern sind. Um keine kostbare Quadratmeter zu verschwenden, ist die Küche optimal auf kleinstem Raum untergebracht. Statt das Apartment mit Kunst zu überfluten, hat der Eigentümer nur einige wenige geschmackvolle Stücke ausgewählt, die stets für Gesprächsstoff sorgen.

Un air distingué imprègne cette demeure de gentilhomme. On trouve un ensemble séjour, cuisine et salle à manger décoré avec un ensemble de pièces dignes d'un musée et des éléments d'ambiance comme des lampes de bronze. Au lieu de prendre des mètres carrés précieux, la cuisine maximise l'espace minimal. Au lieu de surcharger son appartement avec des œuvres d'art, le propriétaire a choisi de mettre en valeur quelques pièces de bon goût.

Un aire refinado se percibe en esta vivienda digna de un caballero. La sala, la cocina y el comedor, forman parte de un solo ambiente decorado con una mezcla de reliquias dignas de museo y estupendos objetos como lámparas de bronce fundido. En vez de quitar valiosos metros cuadrados, la cocina maximiza el mínimo espacio. En lugar de sobrecargar el apartamento con arte, su dueño despliega una variada selección de objetos singulares.

Un'aria signorile pervade l'abitazione di questo gentiluomo caratterizzata da una stanza unica salotto-cucina-pranzo decorata con un cocktail di cimeli da museo e di sofisticati oggetti come lampade in bronzo. Invece di consumare metri quadri preziosi, la cucina fa il massimo uso del minimo spazio. Invece di soffocare l'appartamento di arte, il proprietario mette in mostra alcuni pezzi di ottimo gusto, perfetti per iniziare una conversazione.

Bohemian Treasure

A few blocks from bustling Times Square sits legendary Tiffany & Co. design director's circa-1850, red-brick row house, which he renovated with trademark tasteful elegance. The living room's walls are lined with wildly colorful glass mosaic samples, with a small wooden table topped with Syrian ceramics.

Nur unweit vom belebten Times Square befindet sich das aus rotem Ziegel gebaute, aus der Mitte des 19. Jahrhunderts stammende Stadthaus des legendären Designchefs von Tiffany & Co., das er mit der für ihn typischen geschmackvollen Eleganz renovierte. Die Wände des Wohnzimmers sind mit farbenprächtigen Mustern von Glasmosaiken dekoriert, auf dem kleinen Holztisch befinden sich Keramiken aus Syrien.

À quelques rues de l'effervescence de Times Square, se trouve la célèbre maison en briques rouges datant d'environ 1850, du directeur de design chez Tiffany and Co, qu'il avait rénové avec cette élégance de bon goût qui caractérise la marque. Les murs du salon sont décorés de panneaux de mosaïques en verre aux couleurs éclatantes et une petite table en bois surmontée de céramiques de Syrie.

A pochi isolati dall'animata Times Square sorge la casa di mattoni rossi del direttore del design di Tiffany & Co, la leggendaria gioielleria. L'edificio in cui si trova l'abitazione, che Loring ha ristrutturato con il suo stile raffinato e inconfondibile, risale al 1850 circa. Le pareti del soggiorno sono coperte da coloratissimi mosaici di vetro, mentre su un tavolino di legno sono in bella mostra numerose ceramiche della Siria.

A pocas cuadras de la bulliciosa Times Square, se enclava una casa adosada de ladrillos rojos, de alrededor de 1850, renovada por el legendario director de diseño de Tiffany & Co., con el gusto y elegancia que lo caracterizan. En la sala destacan las paredes decoradas con coloridas muestras de mosaicos de vidrio y una pequeña mesa de madera con superficie recubierta en cerámica siria.

omment a-t-on osé faire
un film de LOLITA ?
METRO-GOLDWYN-MAYER et SEVEN ARTS PRODUCTIONS
JAMES B. HARRIS
STANLEY KUBRICK
LOLITA
AMES MASON · SHELLEY WINTERS · PETER SELLERS SUE LYON
STANLEY KUBRICK
VLADIMIR NABOKOV
JAMES B. HARRIS
l'AMMALIATRICE
Dietrich
un capolavoro

Sag Harbor Hideaway

Located on the waterfront in the Hamptons' luxe Sag Harbor, designer Lisa Perry's six-bedroom mansion is a vibrant mod fantasy drenched in eye-popping primary colors, courtesy of canvases from luminaries like Alexander Calder, Frank Stella and Alexander Liberman. The showpiece of the soaring dining room, styled with George Nelson bubble lamps and a sleek Tucker Robbins table, is an exercise pool equipped with jets for swimming against the current.

Im luxuriösen Sag Harbor in den Hamptons besitzt die Designerin Lisa Perry eine Villa mit sechs Schlafzimmern direkt am Meer – eine moderne Fantasie in atemberaubenden Primfarben, die von Bildern von Künstlern wie Alexander Calder, Frank Stella und Alexander Lieberman strahlen. Das Glanzstück des weitläufigen Speisezimmers, das mit Bubble-Lampen von George Nelson und einem Tucker-Robbins-Tisch ausgestattet ist, ist ein Pool mit Düsen, so dass man gegen die Strömung schwimmen kann.

La mansion de six chambres de la designer de mode Lisa Perry est un monde de fantaisie peint de couleurs primaires tape à l'œil avec des toiles offertes par des artistes réputés comme Alexander Calder, Frank Stella et Alexander Liberman. La pièce maitresse de la salle à manger à plafond haut, ornée avec des lampes boules et une table élégante de Tucker Robbins est une piscine pour exercices aquatiques équipée avec des jets pour nager contre le courant.

Situada a orillas del mar en el lujoso Sag Harbor de Hampton, la mansión de seis dormitorios de la diseñadora Lisa Perry representa una vibrante fantasía moderna impregnada de sorprendentes colores primarios, que surgen de los lienzos de genios como Alexander Calder, Frank Stella y Alexander Liberman. La joya del imponente comedor, decorado con lámparas burbuja de George Nelson y una elegante mesa Tucker Robbins, es una piscina equipada con chorros para nado contracorriente.

Situata sul lungomare della lussuosa Sag Harbor, nella zona delle Hamptons, la residenza della designer Lisa Perry, con le sue sei stanze da letto, è una vivace fantasia alla moda imbevuta di colori primari sfavillanti, grazie alle tele di luminari quali Alexander Calder, Frank Stella e Alexander Liberman. Il pezzo centrale dell'altissima sala da pranzo, adornata da lampade a bolla di George Nelson e da un elegante tavolo di Tucker Robbins, è una piscina attrezzata con getti d'acqua per nuotare contro la corrente.

THE HAMPTONS . Sag Harbor Hideaway 195

The Barnyard

In the Hamptons, a former barnyard was reborn as a banker's spacious summertime retreat. The soaring, sun-soaked dwelling is a marriage of new and old, with glass-floored passageways connecting rooms and the barn's numerous windows reset in steel. The towering, 20-foot-high space is emphasized by the fieldstone fireplace, which climbs to the ceiling. A cantilevered balcony outfitted with a red-leather chaise overlooks the lushly manicured lawn and a 70-foot-long trapezoidal pool that seems to extend into the horizon.

In den Hamptons wurde ein früherer Bauernhof in eine geräumige Sommeroase eines Bankiers umfunktioniert. Dieses majestätische, lichtdurchflutete Gebäude ist eine Symbiose von Alt und Neu. Die Böden der Verbindungszimmer bestehen aus Glas und die zahlreichen Fenster der Scheune haben Stahlrahmen. Die Höhe dieses 7 m hohen Raums wird durch einen mit Stein verkleideten, bis zur Decke reichenden Kamin betont. Von dem weit auskragenden Balkon mit einer roten Leder-Chaiselongue blickt man auf den gepflegten Rasen und einen über 20 m langen, trapezförmigen Pool, der bis zum Horizont zu reichen scheint.

Dans les Hamptons, une ancienne ferme s'est transformée en la résidence d'été spacieuse d'un banquier. Ce bâtiment élancé et inondé de soleil allie le moderne et l'ancien avec des corridors dont le sol est en verre, pour faire communiquer les pièces, et les nombreuses fenêtres de la ferme qui ont été refaites en acier. Cet espace qui s'élèvent à presque 7 m est rehaussé par une cheminée en pierre de taille qui monte jusqu'au plafond. Un balcon en porte-à-faux orné d'un fauteuil en cuir rouge donne sur une pelouse impeccable et une piscine en forme de trapèze de près de 20 mètres de long qui semble se fondre dans l'horizon.

En los Hamptons, un antiguo corral se convirtió en el amplio refugio de verano de un banquero. La altísima y muy iluminada vivienda es un maridaje entre lo nuevo y lo viejo: sus pasillos, con pisos vidriados, que conectan las habitaciones, y las numerosas ventanas del corral enmarcadas en acero. El imponente espacio de 7 metros de alto está resaltado por la chimenea de piedra, que llega hasta el techo. Un balcón voladizo decorado con una tumbona de cuero rojo da hacia una piscina trapezoidal de más de 20 metros que parece perderse en el horizonte, rodeada de un frondoso y bien cuidado césped.

Nella zona delle Hamptons, un ex granaio è stato fatto rinascere e diventare lo spazioso rifugio estivo di un banchiere. Questa svettante casa immersa in un bagno di sole è un connubio di vecchio e nuovo, con corridoi pavimentati in vetro tra le varie stanze e le numerose finestre del vecchio granaio ristrutturate in acciaio. L'ambiente, alto 7 metri, è messo in evidenza da un camino in pietra che sale fino al soffitto. Un balcone aggettante attrezzato con una sedia in pelle rossa si affaccia su un curatissimo prato rigoglioso e su una piscina trapezoidale di oltre 20 etri che sembra estendersi fino all'orizzonte.

Creative Space

In upstate New York, artist Marina Abramović resides on a 26-acre spread containing a river, vegetable garden and an unconventional wooden home modeled after a six-pointed star designed by architect Dennis Wedlick. This unusual shape creates a dizzying, circular layout with certain rooms featuring 360-degree views. The pastoral estate's eclectic home deviates from the rustic-country clichés.

Die Künstlerin Marina Abramović lebt nördlich von New York City auf einem 10 Hektar großen Anwesen mit Fluss, Gemüsegarten und einem unkonventionellen Holzhaus, das einem sechsstrahligen Stern nachempfunden wurde entworfen von dem Architekten Dennis Wedlick. Durch diese ungewöhnliche Form entsteht ein verwirrender, kreisförmiger Grundriss mit Rundumsicht von einigen Zimmern aus. Das eklektische Wohnhaus des Anwesens weicht völlig von den rustikal-ländlichen Klischees ab.

Dans la partie nord de l'état de New York, l'artiste Marina Abramović réside dans un espace de 10 hectares comprenant une rivière, un jardin potager et une maison de bois peu conventionnelle ayant la forme d'une étoile à six branches Conçu par l'architecte Dennis Wedlick. Cette structure inhabituelle créé un agencement circulaire et extravagant avec certaines pièces offrant une vue à 360 degrés. Cette maison pastorale éclectique dans un grand domaine diffère des clichés rustiques traditionnels.

En el norte del estado de Nueva York, la artista Marina Abramović reside en una finca de 10 hectáreas con su propio río, un huerto y una original casa de madera que sigue el patrón de una estrella de seis puntas diseñado por el arquitecto Dennis Wedlick. Esta forma fuera de lo común crea una distribución circular vertiginosa gracias a la cual algunas habitaciones ofrecen vistas de 360 grados. La ecléctica casa de esta bucólica finca se aparta de los clichés campestres.

L'artista Marina Abramović risiede nella zona settentrionale dello stato di New York, su un terreno di circa 10 ettari su cui scorre un fiume, cresce un orto, e sorge una casa in legno dall'aspetto insolito ispirata ad una stella a sei punte porgéttato dall'architetto Dennis Wedlick. Questa forma inconsueta crea una pianta circolare da capogiro, in cui alcune stanze hanno una vista a 360 gradi. Questa eclettica abitazione, seppur situata in una zona rurale, si discosta dai classici clichés del rustico di campagna.

UPSTATE NEW YORK . Creative Space   211

Reto Guntli, photographer

Swiss photographer Reto Guntli travels to all continents reporting on architecture, interiors, people, art, design, travel, and gardens. Having photographed and produced 30 coffee table books for the largest publishing houses in the world, his watchful eye on international cities and their lifestyles is known all over. He regularly contributes to dozens of the most prestigious international magazines such as *Architectural Digest, Vogue, Elle Decor, Condé Nast Traveler, Hotel & Lodges, Geo* and many others. Reto Guntli is also known for his advertising shoots for international hotels and has published several books on the best hotels, resorts and spas around the globe. He is based in Zurich, Switzerland and is represented by zapaimages (www.zapaimages.com).

Der Schweizer Fotograf Reto Guntli bereist alle Kontinente und berichtet über Architektur, Inneneinrichtung, Menschen, Kunst, Design, Reisen und Gärten. Für die größten Verlage der Welt hat er seine Aufnahmen in 30 Bildbänden veröffentlicht. Sein wachsames Auge, das auf internationale Städte und deren Lebensstil gerichtet ist, ist somit überall bekannt. In Dutzenden der angesehensten internationalen Zeitschriften wie *Architectural Digest, Vogue, Elle Decor, Condé Nast Traveler, Hotel & Lodges, Geo* und viele andere werden seine Beiträge regelmäßig veröffentlicht. Darüber hinaus ist Reto Guntli für seine Werbeaufnahmen für internationale Hotels bekannt. Er hat auch mehrere Bücher über die besten Hotels, Resorts und Spas rund um die Welt veröffentlicht. Er ist in Zürich beheimatet und wird von zapaimages (www.zapaimages.com) vertreten.

Le photographe suisse, Reto Guntli, voyage sur tous les continents pour écrire sur l'.architecture, les intérieurs, les gens, l'art, le design, les voyages et les jardins. Ayant photographié et produits 30 beaux livres pour les plus grandes maisons d'édition du monde, son œil averti sur les villes internationales et leur art de vivre est connu partout. Il contribue régulièrement dans des douzaines de magasines internationaux parmi les plus prestigieux comme *Architectural Digest, Vogue, Elle Decor, Condé Nast Traveler, Hotel & Lodges, Géo* et beaucoup d'autres. Reto Guntli est également connu pour ses spots publicitaires pour les hôtels internationaux et il a publié plusieurs livres sur les meilleurs hôtels, villes de plage et spas de toute la planète. Il est basé à Zurich, en Suisse et il est représenté par zapaimages (www.zapaimages.com).

El fotógrafo suizo Reto Guntli viaja por todos los continentes haciendo notas sobre arquitectura, interiorismo, gente, arte, diseño, viajes y jardines. Luego de haber participado en la fotografía y en la producción de 30 libros ilustrados de gran tamaño para las más grandes editoriales del mundo, su conocimiento de las ciudades internacionales y de sus estilos de vida es públicamente reconocido. Es un colaborador frecuente de decenas de las más prestigiosas revistas internacionales tales como *Architectural Digest, Vogue, Elle Decor, Condé Nast Traveler, Hotel & Lodges, Geo* y muchas otras. A Reto Guntli también se lo conoce por sus fotografías publicitarias para hoteles internacionales y ha publicado varios libros sobre los mejores hoteles, resorts y spas en todo el mundo. Reside en Zurich, Suiza y lo representa zapaimages (www.zapaimages.com).

Il fotografo svizzero Reto Guntli viaggia in tutto il mondo facendo servizi su architettura, interni, persone, arte, design, viaggi e giardini. Avendo prodotto 30 libri di fotografie da lui scattate per le più importanti case editrici del mondo, il suo occhio attento alle città internazionali e al loro stile di vita è noto a tutti. Contribuisce regolarmente a decine di prestigiose riviste internazionali quali *Architectural Digest, Vogue, Elle Decor, Condé Nast Traveler, Hotel & Lodges, Geo* e molte altre. Reto Guntli è anche famoso per i suoi servizi pubblicitari per alberghi internazionali ed ha pubblicato diversi libri sui migliori alberghi, centri di villeggiatura e centri benessere del mondo. Vive a Zurigo, in Svizzera, ed è rappresentato da zapaimages (www.zapaimages.com).

Agi Simoes

Brazilian photographer Agi Simoes is based in Zurich, Switzerland and is an international photographer of interiors, architecture, and portraiture for magazines such as *Casa Vogue, Architectural Digest, Elle Decor* and many others. He has also published lifestyle books on Rio de Janeiro, artists in Brazil, Buenos Aires, and Majorca. He often travels and collaborates with Reto Guntli on extensive book and reportage projects.

Der brasilianische Fotograf Agi Simoes hat sein Lager in Zürich aufgeschlagen. Er fotografiert Inneneinrichtung, Architektur und Portraits für Zeitschriften wie *Casa Vogue, Architectural Digest, Elle Decor* und viele andere. Außerdem hat er Bücher über den Lebensstil in Rio de Janeiro, Künstler in Brasilien, Buenos Aires und Mallorca veröffentlicht. Er reist oft mit Reto Guntli und arbeitet mit ihm an umfangreichen Buch- und Reportageprojekten zusammen.

Le photographe brésilien Agi Simoes est basé à Zurich, en Suisse et il est photographe international spécialisé dans les intérieurs, l'architecture et les portraits pour des magasines comme *Casa Vogue, Architectural Digest, Elle Decor* et beaucoup d'autres. Il a également publié des livres sur l'art de vivre à Rio de Janeiro, les artistes du Brésil, Buenos Aires et Majorque. Il voyage souvent et collabore avec Reto Guntli sur des grands projets de livres et reportages.

El fotógrafo brasileño Agi Simoes está radicado en Zurich, Suiza y es un fotógrafo internacional de interiores, arquitectura y retratos para revistas como *Casa Vogue, Architectural Digest, Elle Decor* y muchas otras. También publicó libros sobre el estilo de vida en Río de Janeiro, Buenos Aires y Mallorca. Suele viajar y colaborar con Reto Guntli en grandes proyectos de libros y reportajes.

Il fotografo brasiliano Agi Simoes vive a Zurigo, in Svizzera, ed è un fotografo di interni, di architettura e di ritrattistica di fama internazionale. Collabora con riviste come *Casa Vogue, Architectural Digest, Elle Decor* e molte altre. Ha anche pubblicato libri di stile di vita su Rio de Janeiro e su artisti brasiliani, di Buenos Aires e di Majorca. Viaggia spesso e collabora con Reto Guntli per libri e reportage di ampio respiro.

Josh Bernstein, Writer

Joshua M. Bernstein is a Brooklyn-based journalist and critic who writes about food, drinks, culture, and architecture for *ReadyMade, Forbes Traveler, Gourmet.com,* the *New York Press* and, in a moment of weakness, *Dolls Magazine.* He spends his days pedaling his trusty 10-speed bike around New York City, searching for oddball characters, crisp pork-and-chive dumplings, cool pints of properly poured beer, and bars that are as frightening as their drinks are strong. He can be reached at josh.bernstein@gmail.com.

Joshua M. Bernstein ist ein in Brooklyn ansässiger Journalist und Kritiker, der für *ReadyMade, Forbes Traveler, Gourmet.com,* die *New York Press* und in einem Moment der Schwäche für *Dolls Magazine* über Essen, Getränke, Kultur und Architektur schreibt. Tagsüber fährt er auf seinem altbewährten Zehn-Gang-Rad durch New York City und sucht nach merkwürdigen Gestalten, knusprigen, mit Schweinefleisch und Schnittlauch gefüllten chinesischen Klößen, erfrischende, gut gezapfte Biere und Bars, die ebenso erschreckend sind wie ihre Drinks stark. Zu erreichen ist er unter josh.bernstein@gmail.com.

Joshua M. Bernstein est un journaliste et critique basé à Brooklyn qui écrit sur la nourriture, les boissons, la culture et l'architecture pour *ReadyMade, Forbes Traveler, Gourmet.com,* le *New York Press* et dans un moment de faiblesse, *Dolls Magazine.* Il passe ses journées à pédaler sur sa fidèle bicyclette à 10 vitesses autour de la ville de New York, à la recherche de personnages originaux, de raviolis à croquer au porc et câpres, des pintes de bière pression bien fraiche et des bars qui intimident avec leurs mélanges très forts. On peut le joindre à josh.bernstein@gmail.com.

Joshua M. Bernstein, que reside en Brooklyn, es un periodista y crítico gastronómico, de cultura y arquitectura que escribe para *ReadyMade, Forbes Traveler, Gourmet.com, New York Press* y, en un momento de debilidad, para *Dolls Magazine.* Pasa los días pedaleando en su fiel bicicleta de 10 velocidades a través de Nueva York, en la búsqueda de personajes excéntricos, de crocantes dumplings rellenos de cerdo y cebolletas, de cerveza helada bien servida y de aterradores bares que sirven los tragos más fuertes. Se lo puede contactar a través de su dirección de correo electrónico josh.bernstein@gmail.com.

Joshua M. Bernstein, giornalista e critico che vive a Brooklyn, scrive di cibo, drink, cultura e architettura per *ReadyMade, Forbes Traveler, Gourmet.com, New York Press* e, in momenti di debolezza, per *Dolls Magazine.* Trascorre le sue giornate pedalando la sua fedele bicicletta a 10 marce per tutta New York, alla ricerca di personaggi stravaganti, di croccanti gnocchetti di maiale ed erba cipollina, di fresche pinte di birra versata nel modo giusto, e di pub spaventosi dove assaggiare drink fortissimi. È possibile raggiungerlo all'indirizzo elettronico josh.bernstein@gmail.com.

CREDITS

Skyline Views

(Title not given) © 2010 Estate of Pablo Picasso / Artists Rights Society (ARS), New York (p. 18)

Upper East Side Luxury

Interior design by artist/sculptor Pascale Gallais Agostinelli. www.pascalegallaissculptor.com

Sutton Place Penthouse

Interior design by Ingrao, Inc. *Interior with Built-in Bar,* 1991 © Estate of Roy Lichtenstein (p. 3, p. 45) | (Title not given) © 2010 The Andy Warhol Foundation for the Visual Arts, Inc. / Artists Rights Society (ARS), New York (p. 46) | (Title not given) © Bridget Riley 2010. All rights reserved. Courtesy Karsten Schubert, London (p. 47) | Victor Vasarely (Title not given) © 2010 Artists Rights Society (ARS), New York / ADAGP, Paris (p. 48, p. 50)

Townhouse Uptown

The Wedding photograph © 1994 Sandy Skoglund (p. 55) | (Title not given) © Justen Ladda (p. 56) | *Glow in the Dark* © Al Souza (p. 57) | (Title not given) © Iris Binor (p. 57) | (Title not given) © Bruce Pearson. www.brucepearson.com (p. 59) | (Title not given) © 2010 The Andy Warhol Foundation for the Visual Arts, Inc. / Artists Rights Society (ARS), New York (p. 59) | (Title not given) © Neil Winokur. Courtesy of Janet Borden, Inc. (p. 6, p. 61) | (Title not given) © Justen Ladda (p. 62)

Upper East Side Studio

Interior design by Giuseppe Pica | (Title not given) © Jack Sonnenberg (p. 65, p. 67) | (Title not given) © Dan Content (p. 66) | (Title not given) © Tajiri Shinchiki (p. 66) | (Title not given) © Jerry Okimoto (pp. 68–69, p. 70)

Harlem Grandeur

Interior design by Wagner Van Dam, Design and Decoration

Uptown Residence

(Title not given) © Nicola de Maria. Courtesy of Galerie Lelong, Paris (p. 87) | (Title not given) © A.R. Penck. Courtesy of Michael Werner Gallery (pp. 88–89) | (Title not given) © Ursula Hodel (p. 90) | (Title not given) © Nicola de Maria. Courtesy of Galerie Lelong, Paris (p. 91) | (Title not given) © Ursula Hodel (p. 91) | Diego Giacometti (Title not given) © 2010 Artists Rights Society (ARS), New York / ADAGP, Paris (p. 91) | Art © Louise Bourgeois / Licensed by VAGA, New York, NY (p. 91)

Sumptuous Uptown

Interior design by Carlo Rampazzi | (Title not given) © Lovka Photography (p. 101)

Upper East Side Elegance

Interior design by Ingrao, Inc.

Upper East Side Vintage

Photograph (Title not given) © Estate of Herbert Matter / Swiss foundation for Photography, Winterthur, Switzerland (p. 117) | (Title not given) © Antonio López (p. 117)

Garment District Loft

(Title not given) © Jeff Lewis.
www.jefflewis.com
(pp. 123–125)

Gramercy Park Treasure

(Title not given) © Ryo Toyonaga (p. 131, p. 137) |
(Title not given) Copyright © Lee Bontecou /
courtesy Knoedler & Company (pp. 136–137)

Downtown Residence

Interior design by Ingrao, Inc. | (Title not given)
© Robert Barry. Used with permission from the
artist. Permission obtained with help from
Deborah Colton Gallery (pp. 147–148) |
(Title not given) © Red Grooms / Artists Rights
Society (ARS), New York (p. 151) | (Title not given)
© Ed Ruscha (p. 150, p. 153) | (Title not given)
© 2010 Man Ray Trust / Artists Rights Society
(ARS), New York / ADAGP, Paris (p. 153)

Soho Loft

Untitled (Black Folds I) & *Untitled (Black Folds V),*
2005. Iran do Espírito Santo. Permanent marker
on paper. © Iran do Espírito Santo, Courtesy:
Sean Kelly Gallery, New York (p. 156) |
Untitled, 1986–1987. Antony Gormley.
Graphite and oil on paper. © Antony Gormley,
Courtesy: Sean Kelly Gallery, New York (p. 159) |
Blind Stars, Bette Davis, 2002. Douglas Gordon.
Gelatin silver print. © Douglas Gordon. Courtesy
Gagosian Gallery (p. 159) | *Untitled,* 1947. Louise
Bourgeois. Ink on paper. © Louise Bourgeois /
Licensed by VAGA, New York, NY (p. 159) |
Joseph Beuys (Title not given) © 2010 Artists
Rights Society (ARS), New York / VG Bild-Kunst,

Bonn (p. 159) | *Untitled,* 1978. Jannis Kounellis.
Pencil and charcoal on paper. © Jannis Kounellis,
Courtesy Ace Gallery (p. 159) | *England,* 1968.
Richard Long. Vintage silver print. © Richard Long
(p. 159) | *Never, never (white),* 2000.
Douglas Gordon. Digital print on C-type paper.
© Douglas Gordon. Courtesy Gagosian Gallery
(p. 159) | *Never, never (black),* 2000. Douglas
Gordon. Digital print on C-type paper.
© Douglas Gordon. Courtesy Gagosian Gallery
(p. 159) | L.H.O.O.Q. Marcel Duchamp © 2010
Artists Rights Society (ARS), New York / ADAGP,
Paris / Succession Marcel Duchamp (p. 160) |
Untitled, 1957. Yves Klein. Pigment on wood.
© 2010 Artists Rights Society (ARS),
New York / ADGAP, Paris (p. 161)

Soho Minimalist

Dennis Wedlick Architect LLC

Mid-Century Dwelling

Interior design by Rudy Guerrino

Chelsea Apartment

Interior Design by Dartoma Design

Sag Harbor Hideaway

Interior design by Ingrao, Inc. | *Egg on Plate
with Knife, Fork, and Spoon,* 1964. Alex Hay.
Spray acrylic and stencil on linen; painted
fiberglass; in four panels, 86 × 140¼ × 6¾
inches (218.4 × 356.2 × 17.1 cm) © Alex Hay.
Courtesy of Peter Freeman, Inc. (p. 189) |
(Title not given) © 2010 Frank Stella / Artists
Rights Society (ARS), New York (p. 192) |
Art © The Leon Polk Smith Foundation /

Other titles by teNeues

ISBN 978-3-8327-9309-8

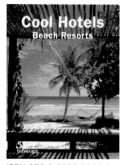

ISBN 978-3-8327-9274-9

ISBN 978-3-8327-9398-2

ISBN 978-3-8327-9247-3

ISBN 978-3-8327-9234-3

ISBN 978-3-8327-9308-1

ISBN 978-3-8327-9243-5

ISBN 978-3-8327-9230-5

ISBN 978-3-8327-9396-8

Size: **15 x 19 cm**, 6 x 7 ½ in., 224 pp., **Flexicover**, c. 200 color photographs,
Text: English / German / French / Spanish / Italian
www.teneues.com

Other titles by teNeues

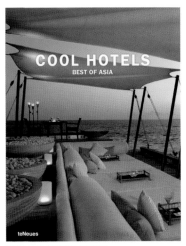

ISBN 978-3-8327-9238-1

ISBN 978-3-8327-9235-0

Size: **25.6 x 32.6 cm**, 10 x 12⁷/₈ in., 396 pp., **Hardcover with jacket**, c. 650 color photographs,
Text: English / German / French / Spanish / Italian

www.teneues.com

teNeues' new Cool Guide series

ISBN 978-3-8327-9293-0

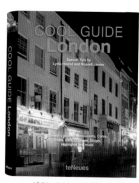

ISBN 978-3-8327-9294-7

ISBN 978-3-8327-9295-4

ISBN 978-3-8327-9296-1

ISBN 978-3-8327-9236-7

ISBN 978-3-8327-9202-2

Size: **15 x 19 cm**, 6 x 7 ½ in., 224 pp., **Flexicover**, c. 250 color photographs,
Text: English / German / French / Spanish
www.teneues.com